Life Around the World
Transport in Many Cultures

Martha EH Rustad

raintree

a Capstone company — publishers for children

Raintree is an imprint of Capstone Global Library Limited, a company incorporated in England and Wales having its registered office at 264 Banbury Road, Oxford, OX2 7DY – Registered company number: 6695582

www.raintree.co.uk
myorders@raintree.co.uk

Edited by Sarah L Schuette
Designed by Kim Brown and Alison Thiele
Picture research by Wanda Winch
Originated by Capstone Global Library Ltd
Printed and bound in China

ISBN 978 1 4747 3538 4
20 19 18 17 16
10 9 8 7 6 5 4 3 2 1

British Library Cataloguing in Publication Data
A full catalogue record for this book is available from the British Library.

Acknowledgements
Capstone Studio: Karon Dubke, 9; Getty Images: Opus/a.collectionRF, 7; Shutterstock: Adisa, Cover, Anton_Ivanov, 21, cowardlion, 11, gary718, 1, imagestockdesign, 13, Ivan Cholakov, 17, Melissa King, 19, thieury, 5, Thorsten Rust, 15

Every effort has been made to contact copyright holders of material reproduced in this book. Any omissions will be rectified in subsequent printings if notice is given to the publisher.

Contents

Transport 4

Going to school. 6

Going to other places 14

On the go! 20

Glossary 22

Find out more 23

Websites 23

Index 24

Transport

People travel
in every culture.
Let's see how other people
around the world travel.

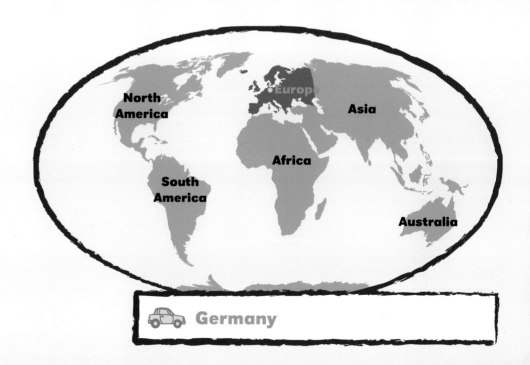

Going to school

These girls in China
walk to school.

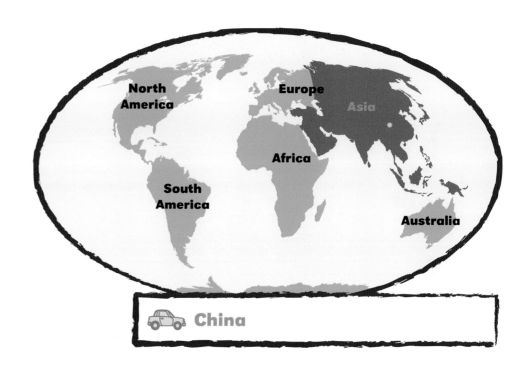

These boys in
the United States
go to school by bus.

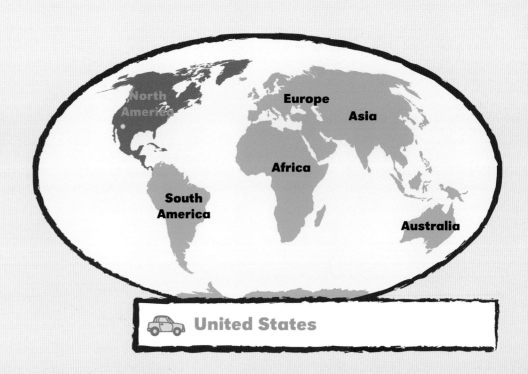

United States

These girls in Japan
go to school by train.

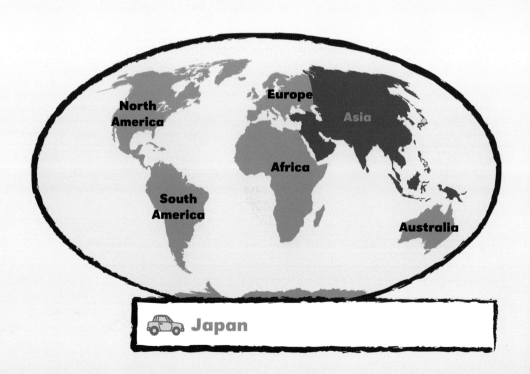

North
America

Europe

Asia

Africa

South
America

Australia

Japan

These kids in Cambodia
paddle boats to get
to their floating school.

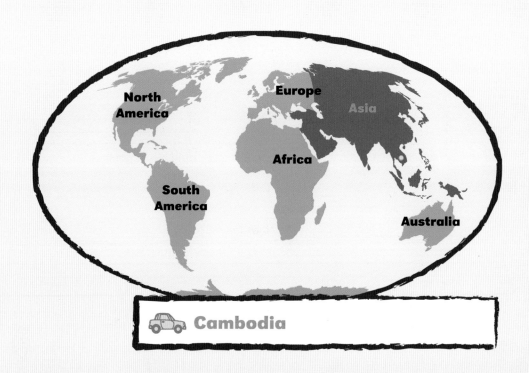

Going to other places

People in Australia

travel by monorail.

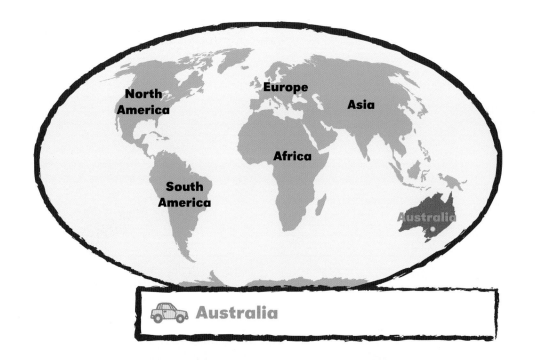

Australia

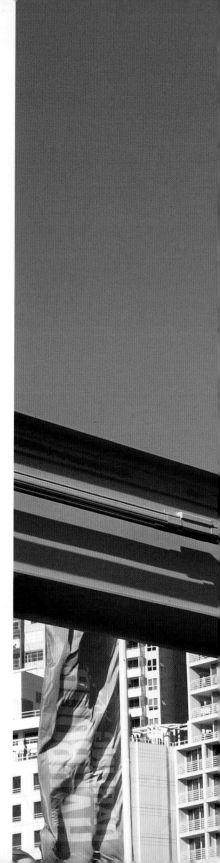

Travellers in Bolivia

take an aeroplane

to another country.

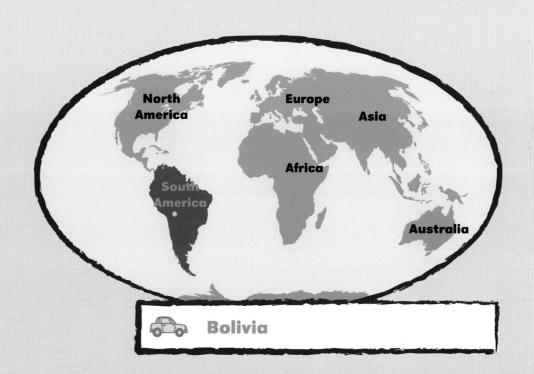

North
America

Europe

Asia

Africa

South
America

Australia

Bolivia

A boy in Canada

rides a snowmobile.

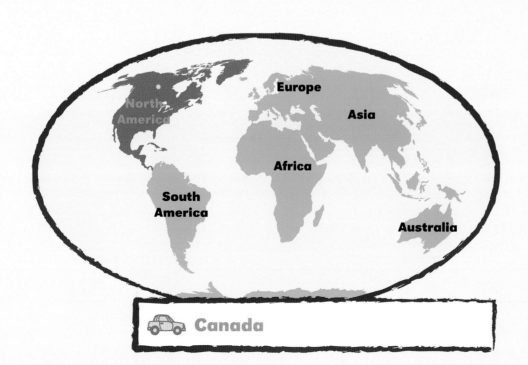

North America

Europe

Asia

Africa

South America

Australia

Canada

On the go!

Around the world,

people travel on buses,

bicycles and animals.

How will you travel today?

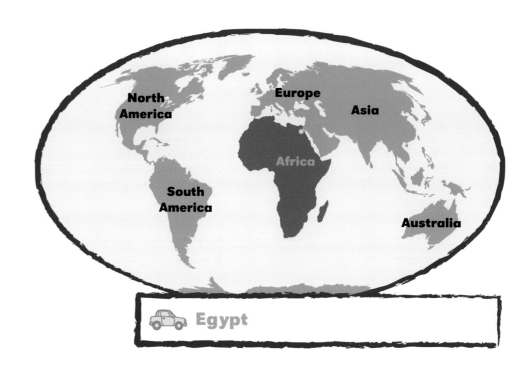

Glossary

culture   way of life, ideas, customs and traditions of a group of people

monorail   train that runs on one rail, usually high above the ground

paddle   push through the water with an oar

snowmobile   vehicle with skis used to travel over snow

travel   go from one place to another

Find out more

How We Get Around (My World Your World), Ellen Lawrence (Ruby Tuesday Books, 2015)

My First Book of Transport, Charlotte Guillain (A&C Black, 2012)

Transport Around the World (Children Like Us), Moira Butterfield (Wayland, 2016)

Websites

http://easyscienceforkids.com/all-about-transportation/
Fun facts about different types of transport.

http://www.bbc.co.uk/education/topics/zt2mn39/videos/1
Videos about different methods of transport around the world.

Index

aeroplanes   16

animals   20

Australia   14

bicycles   20

boats   12

Bolivia   16

buses   8, 20

Cambodia   12

Canada   18

China   6

cultures   4

Japan   10

monorails   14

school   6, 8, 10, 12

snowmobiles   18

trains   10

United States   8

walking   6